A Robbie Reader

What's So Great About...?

POCAHONTAS

Susan Sales Harkins and
William H. Harkins

South Huntington Pub. Lib.
145 Pidgeon Hill Rd.
Huntington Sta., N.Y. 11746

P.O. Box 196
Hockessin, Delaware 19707
Visit us on the web: www.mitchelllane.com
Comments? email us: mitchelllane@mitchelllane.com

Mitchell Lane PUBLISHERS

Copyright © 2009 by Mitchell Lane Publishers. All rights reserved. No part of this book may be reproduced without written permission from the publisher. Printed and bound in the United States of America.

Printing   1   2   3   4   5   6   7   8   9

A Robbie Reader/What's So Great About . . . ?

Amelia Earhart	Anne Frank	Annie Oakley
Christopher Columbus	Daniel Boone	Davy Crockett
The Donner Party	Elizabeth Blackwell	Ferdinand Magellan
Francis Scott Key	Galileo	George Washington Carver
Harriet Tubman	Helen Keller	Henry Hudson
Jacques Cartier	Johnny Appleseed	King Tut
Lewis and Clark	Martin Luther King Jr.	Paul Bunyan
Pocahontas	Robert Fulton	Rosa Parks
Sam Houston		

Library of Congress Cataloging-in-Publication Data
Harkins, Susan Sales.
  Pochantas / by Susan Sales Harkins and William H. Harkins.
     p. cm. — (A Robbie reader) (What's so great about...?)
  Includes bibliographical references and index.
  ISBN 978-1-58415-682-6 (library bound)
  1. Pocahontas, d. 1617—Juvenile literature. 2. Powhatan women—Biography—Juvenile literature. 3. Smith, John, 1580–1631—Juvenile literature. 4. Rolfe, John, 1585–1622—Juvenile literature. I. Harkins, William H. II. Title.
  E99.P85P573657 2009
  975.5'01092—dc22
  [B]
                                                                                                        2008020901

ABOUT THE AUTHORS: Susan and William Harkins live in Kentucky, where they enjoy writing together for children. Susan has written many books for adults and children. William is a history buff. In addition to writing, he is a member of the Air National Guard. They have written over a dozen nonfiction books for Mitchell Lane Publishers.

AUTHORS' NOTE: The story of Pocahontas is just that—a story. Captain John Smith is the only contemporary person to have written extensively about her friendship with the English colonists at Jamestown, and many historians note that Smith would often exaggerate. Other than what Smith mentions in his writings, we don't know any details about her life or the conversations she had with her family or with the colonists. What she said and felt about events is not known with any certainty.

  The events in this story are based on extensive research on the Powhatan nation, archaeological findings, and primary sources, such as Smith's diaries and books. The story represents what may or could have happened and tells, from the perspective of Pocahontas, what we know about her life. We know that she visited the fort, and a few colonists wrote in their diaries that she and Smith were friendly. We know from diary accounts that she brought food to the colonists many times. It is important to note that the modern Powhatan nation refutes Smith's story that Pocahontas saved him from certain death.

PUBLISHER'S NOTE: The following story has been thoroughly researched and to the best of our knowledge represents a true story. While every possible effort has been made to ensure accuracy, the publisher will not assume liability for damages caused by inaccuracies in the data, and makes no warranty on the accuracy of the information contained herein.

PLB

TABLE OF CONTENTS

Chapter One
Strangers! 5

Chapter Two
A Legend 9

Chapter Three
New Friendships 13

Chapter Four
Kidnapped! 19

Chapter Five
Pocahontas in England 25

Chronology 28
Timeline in History 29
Find Out More 30
    Books 30
    Works Consulted 30
    On the Internet 31
Glossary 31
Index 32

Words in **bold** type can be found in the glossary.

English settlers build Fort James. In December of 1606, a group of brave adventurers left England for the New World. They crossed the Atlantic in three small ships, the *Discovery*, the *Godspeed*, and the *Susan Constant*. After almost four months at sea, the colonists spotted land—what we know today as the Chesapeake Bay area. Unseen by the Englishmen, native people watched the ships sail up the river.

CHAPTER ONE

Strangers!

Pocahontas (poh-kah-HON-tus) spotted her father ahead. "Father! Father! My brother has news of the white men!" she shouted. Powhatan (POW-ah-tan) was the great chief of the Powhatan people.

Pocahontas returned her father's quick smile. Then the old man greeted his son, who was also a chief.

"Father, I met the white men," her brother said. "They came ashore and our women cooked a feast. Newport is their chief's name. England is their home across the sea. They are rich. They left many gifts. These strange men seem friendly, but a gun on their boat makes a noise as loud as thunder!"

CHAPTER ONE

At first, Fort James was just a few huts and tents. After a local tribe attacked the settlers, the Englishmen built a wall around their settlement.

"This is good news. We should make these strangers our friends," her father said.

Weeks before, Pocahontas had heard of the strangers who floated up and down the great river in three big boats. Why had they come? she wondered.

When the corn sprouted, the white men moved to a small island. They named their new

STRANGERS!

home Fort James. Pocahontas wasn't afraid of the white men, but she was curious. Animals and mosquitoes lived on that island, but not people. She wondered why the white men had chosen such a dreadful place to live.

By the time the corn was tall, most of the strangers were ill. Many died from drinking germy water. Some of her people thought the white men were starving. Why did they stay inside their fort instead of hunting and fishing? Pocahontas wondered.

That summer was dry. Corn wilted in the fields. After the small harvest, the Englishmen traded beads, **copper**, and farming tools for food. Pocahontas heard that one of the white chiefs, John Smith, was a fair trader. After trading, he left each village with many **bushels** of corn for his people.

Near their villages, the Powhatans grew maize (corn) and other vegetables. There were about 14,000 Powhatans in the Chesapeake Bay area when the English settlers arrived.

Pocahontas Saving the Life of Captain John Smith. No portrait exists of Pocahontas as a child. From diaries, we know that she was small and thin, but not sickly or frail. Many portraits show Pocahontas as a young woman saving John Smith, perhaps to illustrate the romance the two never had. According to Smith, she was about eleven when they met and she supposedly saved his life.

CHAPTER TWO

A Legend

As was the custom with their people, Powhatan had several wives. At eleven years old, Pocahontas helped her many stepmothers prepare for Smith's visit.

"Fetch fresh water!"

"Collect more firewood!"

"Pound more corn! We will need many corn cakes for the feast Powhatan has ordered."

When she finished, Pocahontas sat on a grass mat at her father's feet. **Elders** and **warriors** stood behind him. There was plenty of room for everyone. Her father's roundhouse was the largest in the village. It took the bark of many trees to line the walls.

9

CHAPTER TWO

"Haaamp!" the crowd shouted as Smith entered her father's house.

Pocahontas stared at Smith. Red hair covered his face and head. She'd never seen that much hair on a man's face. Then she looked up at her father. Pocahontas felt safe. She knew she was his favorite child. He never called her by her real name, Amonute. *Pocahontas* was a nickname he used to tease her. It meant "naughty girl."

Around his neck, Powhatan wore many chains of pearls. A robe of raccoon skins warmed his shoulders. Surely, Smith would see how rich and powerful her father was, she thought.

Powhatan invited Smith to eat. Was Smith an important chief? she wondered. She listened as the elders talked. Some of the elders wanted to kill him!

Pocahontas trembled when her father lifted his hand. Some men brought in two large stones.

"No!" Pocahontas cried.

More men grabbed Smith and pushed him down on the stones.

A LEGEND

"No, father! Don't let them kill him!" she cried. Powhatan ignored her. Pocahontas rushed forward and bent over Smith. "Please, Father, save him!"

Powhatan nodded, and the men released Smith. "We will be friends," Powhatan said to Smith. "I will treat your people as brothers."

"I also promise to treat your people as brothers," Smith replied.

For a while, both men kept their promise.

No one knows if Pocahontas really saved John Smith's life. Smith first told this story many years later, when he was an old man. But we do know that Pocahontas was friendly, curious, and brave. The English fort was about twelve miles from her village, but she took food to the settlers. Because she taught Captain John Smith her language, he was able to trade with her people.

Raccoons and beavers were plentiful when the settlers arrived. Clothing was made from their fur.

John Smith was an English adventurer. His father was a farmer, and Smith received a limited but good education. As a soldier, he fought in Spain and Hungary. He was even a slave to a Turk for a while. By the time he sailed to Jamestown, he was a daring and confident man.

CHAPTER THREE

New Friendships

After that, Pocahontas saw Smith many times. Her father asked Smith why the white men had come.

"We have settled on the river. From our small fort, we want to explore this land. We want to find a river to the ocean in the west," Smith said. That ocean was the Pacific. "For many years, men have hunted for this river. It is the year of our Lord, sixteen hundred and seven. Someone will soon find it. I want to be that man." Pocahontas and the others didn't know what *sixteen hundred and seven* meant.

Powhatan shook his head. "Smith, you are my friend now. I will tell you the truth. No river will take you to the salt sea in the west."

13

CHAPTER THREE

Pocahontas's people lived in rounded huts. They used seedlings that bent easily to make a frame. Then they covered the frame with bark and dried grass. A fire burned in the center. The huts were dark and smoky, but comfortable.

NEW FRIENDSHIPS

After a few days, Powhatan sent Smith home. In return for freeing Smith, Powhatan asked for two **cannons** and a **grindstone**. The guns would make his enemies fear him. The grindstone would help his wives grind corn into flour. Smith agreed to send the items.

The guns were too heavy for Powhatan's men to carry home through the forest. Smith sent beads and copper instead.

A few days later, Powhatan called for Pocahontas. "A fire at the fort has destroyed all their food," he said. "I want you to take food to our new friends."

Pocahontas was excited. She would see the fort and John Smith. After a long journey, she and her people waited at the fort's big wooden door. When it opened, John Smith stepped out. He looked surprised to see her.

"We heard about the fire. We have brought food," she said.

Smith accepted the food gladly and invited them inside the fort. Smith sent her home with beads and copper gifts for her father.

CHAPTER THREE

In 1607, the English settlers built Fort James (now called Jamestown) in what would become Virginia. The Powhatans lived about twelve miles to the north, near the York River. Williamsburg would not be settled until 1633. Richmond grew up from a trading post established in 1637.

NEW FRIENDSHIPS

John Smith Making Toys for Pocahontas. Pocahontas visited John Smith and the other men at the fort many times. Usually, she brought food. Most likely, she saved them from starving to death more than once. Smith admired her lively spirit and gave her the nickname Nonpareil, which is French for "having no equal."

That year, Pocahontas journeyed from the Powhatan village on the York River to Fort James many times. Smith taught her how to speak English. They became good friends.

17

Thanks in part to the friendship between Pocahontas and John Smith, the men at Fort James got along well with most of the Powhatan tribes. The settlers weren't good at growing their own food. They visited Powhatan villages to trade. Many Powhatans visited the settlers at the fort. Not all of the local natives were friendly, though. Just a few weeks after the English arrived, a local tribe attacked them and killed a few of the settlers. It was often dangerous for the white men to leave the fort.

CHAPTER FOUR

Kidnapped!

The harvest was light. No one had any corn to spare. Powhatan refused to trade with Smith. The old chief tried to explain, saying, "There isn't much corn. If we give you corn, we will go hungry this winter."

"You are trying to starve us to death!" Smith yelled at Powhatan.

Smith forced Powhatan to give him many bushels of corn. Powhatan was also angry. He told Pocahontas she could never visit the fort again.

The next spring, Pocahontas heard that many of her friends at the fort had died over the harsh winter. She was sad when she heard that John Smith had also died.

CHAPTER FOUR

Despite the **hardships** at the fort, even more white men came from England. They cut down trees and planted crops. Powhatan grew tired of the English settlers. Pocahontas heard him say that he would force them to leave. His warriors captured many white men and kept them as prisoners. Powhatan took their guns.

Pocahontas knew that her happy days at the fort were over. Her father married her to a brave named Kocoum. As a married woman, she cut her hair short, as was the Powhatan custom.

When she was eighteen, Pocahontas met Samuel Argall. He invited her to visit his ship. Once Pocahontas was on board, Argall sailed for Fort James. He kept her as a prisoner.

Argall made a deal with Powhatan. The old chief must let all the white prisoners go. He must also return all the stolen guns. Only then would Argall send Pocahontas home.

Powhatan sent each of the prisoners home with a broken gun. He didn't return all of the guns, so Argall kept Pocahontas. She was upset. Did her father care more about the white man's

KIDNAPPED!

In 1910, artist Jean Leon Gerome Ferris painted *The Abduction of Pocahontas*. Two of Pocahontas's own people tricked her into boarding the ship of Samuel Argall (who stands at left). For their help, they received a copper kettle.

guns than about her? Some women at the fort gave her English dresses and shoes. She grew her hair long like the English women.

After a few months, Pocahontas moved to Henrico. There, she learned to cook and sew like a white woman. Her captors read to her from their Bible. She learned about the white man's God. In Henrico, she met John Rolfe, an English planter.

CHAPTER FOUR

The Baptism of Pocahontas. Before she could marry John Rolfe, Pocahontas had to be baptized a Christian. At that time, the English settlers hoped to convert the natives to Christians. John Gadsby Chapman's painting of 1840 shows Rolfe standing nearby while Pocahontas's brother turns away in protest. It is believed that their marriage was the first between a Native American and a European.

A year later, Powhatan returned all of the guns. By then, Pocahontas wanted to marry John Rolfe. She agreed to be **baptized** and took the English name Rebecca. When her uncle and brother came to her wedding in 1614, she was happy.

KIDNAPPED!

The Marriage of Pocahontas to John Rolfe. Henry Brueckner was an artist and printmaker. In 1855, he painted his own idea of Pocahontas's wedding ceremony.

The next year, Pocahontas had a baby boy. She and John named him Thomas.

Her marriage changed how the settlers and the Powhatans got along. The marriage of Pocahontas and John Rolfe stopped the fighting between their peoples.

William Ordway Partridge sculpted this statue of Pocahontas in 1922. It is just over six feet tall and stands in historic Jamestown. Like many artists, Partridge did not stick to the facts. The clothing on the statue is not typical of the Powhatan clothing of Pocahontas's time.

23

An engraving by Simon van de Passe, made in 1616, is the only known portrait of Pocahontas. A later oil painting (above), based on the engraving, hangs in the National Portrait Gallery in Washington, D.C. By 1616, Pocahontas was wearing English clothing. While she was in England, many people gave her presents of the latest European fashions.

Pocahontas in England

Pocahontas, her husband, and her son sailed across the ocean to England. They traveled with other colonists and a few members of Pocahontas's family.

In London, Pocahontas saw many houses. They were much larger than those at the fort. People rode through the streets in carriages pulled by horses.

Pocahontas did not like everything about London. Streets were full of garbage. The damp English air made her sick.

Everywhere she went, the English called her Lady Rebecca. Because her father was a

CHAPTER FIVE

great chief, they thought she was a princess. Her people had no princesses. At parties, she watched the English dance. Her people were much more joyful when they danced.

Pocahontas heard that John Smith wasn't dead; he had returned to England. The men at the fort had lied to her.

John Smith visited Pocahontas. She reminded him of his promise to treat her people as brothers.

Before she could return home, Pocahontas became sick, most likely from **tuberculosis** (too-bur-kyoo-LOH-sis) or **pneumonia** (noo-MOH-nyuh). In March of 1617, she died. She was just twenty-one years old. Her husband buried her in Gravesend, England.

Rolfe left his young son in England with his family. Then he returned

Pocahontas and her family sailed to England on a British galleon. This type of ship was also used in battle and for exploring new lands.

26

POCAHONTAS IN ENGLAND

The Sedgeford Portrait of Pocahontas and her son. Thomas, the only child of Pocahontas and John Rolfe, was just two when Pocahontas died. His father left him with family in England. At twenty-one, Thomas returned to Virginia and stayed. By then, John Rolfe was already dead. Thomas never knew either of his famous parents.

to Virginia. Thomas was raised and educated in England. Back in Virginia, Rolfe became an important member of the colony and remarried. He died in 1622.

Today, we enjoy the story of Pocahontas. As a young girl, she was curious about the white men. Without her, the settlers at Fort James would have starved. When she married John Rolfe, everyone tried to live in peace. For a short time, this young girl united the English and her people. Although Pocahontas did not live long enough to see it, the white men changed her world forever.

CHRONOLOGY

1580 John Smith is born in England.
1595 Pocahontas is born as Amonute,* probably in Werowocomoco in what is now Virginia.
1607 White men found Fort James (Jamestown) in Powhatan territory in May. Pocahontas meets John Smith in December. Powhatan and John Smith become friends.
1608 Pocahontas visits Fort James many times. John Smith and Powhatan quarrel over food that winter.
1609 John Smith returns to England in October. The fort catches fire. Men at the fort tell Pocahontas that Smith is dead.
1610 Pocahontas marries Kocoum. John Rolfe arrives in Jamestown.
1613 Captain Samuel Argall kidnaps Pocahontas in April.
1614 Pocahontas marries John Rolfe. History does not reveal why she was no longer married to Kocoum.
1615 Pocahontas and John Rolfe have a son. They name him Thomas.
1616 The Rolfe family sails for England. John Smith and Pocahontas meet one last time in England.
1617 Pocahontas dies in March, while still in England.
1618 Powhatan dies in spring.
1622 In Virginia, John Rolfe dies in March. Historians are unsure of the cause.
1624 John Smith publishes a book about his time in Virginia.
1631 John Smith dies in London, England.
1636 Thomas Rolfe travels to Virginia. He will marry there and have two children.
1646 The Powhatan tribes sign their first treaty with the English settlers at Jamestown.
1651 First Indian reservation is established for Powhatan people.

*Amonute was her given name. Matoaka was her **sacred** name, known only to her, which she did eventually reveal. Sources often confuse these two names.

TIMELINE IN HISTORY

1492	Christopher Columbus arrives in what will be called the Americas.
1521	Hernando Cortés of Spain conquers the Aztecs in Mexico.
c. 1540	Chief Powhatan is born.
1565	The Spanish found St. Augustine in Florida.
1587	John White founds Roanoke Island colony off the coast of Virginia; within three years, the colony mysteriously disappears.
1605	The French found Port Royal in Canada.
1606	King James I of England awards a charter to investors for the Virginia Company of London.
1607	Jamestown is founded as Fort James.
1608	The French found Québec in Canada.
1616	An outbreak of smallpox nearly wipes out the Native American population in New England.
1619	The Virginia House of Burgesses meets for the first time.
1620	The *Mayflower* arrives in New England.
1622	Powhatan Indians kill 347 settlers on March 22.
1623	After negotiating peace with a Powhatan village, Captain William Tucker proposes a toast with a poisonous drink; 200 Native Americans die from the poison, and 50 more are slaughtered.
1624	James I revokes the company charter and takes over Virginia as a royal colony. Dutch settlers found the colony of New Netherland.
1626	Peter Minuit buys Manhattan Island from a Delaware tribe.
1637	At the Mystic Massacre in Connecticut, over 400 Pequots, mostly women and children, are killed.
1664	The British take New Netherland and rename it New York.
1665	The French begin their campaign against the Iroquois in Canada.

FIND OUT MORE

Books

Fritz, Jean. *The Double Life of Pocahontas*. New York: Putnam Juvenile, 2002.

Schaefer, Lola M. *Pocahontas*. Mankato, Minnesota: Capstone Press, 2000.

Sjonger, Rebecca. *Life of the Powhatan*. New York: Crabtree Publishing Company, 2004.

Stiles, Martha Bennett. *One Among the Indians*. Lincoln, Nebraska: iUniverse, Inc., 2006.

Thompson, John. *The Journals of Captain John Smith: A Jamestown Biography*. Washington, D.C.: National Geographic, 2007.

Works Consulted

Barbour, Philip L. *Pocahontas and Her World*. Boston: Houghton Mifflin Company, 1970.

Gleach, Frederic W. *Powhatan's World and Colonial Virginia*. Lincoln: The University of Nebraska Press, 1997.

Lemay, J. A. Leo. *Did Pocahontas Save Captain John Smith?* Athens, Georgia: The University of Georgia Press, 1992.

Mossiker, Frances. *Pocahontas: The Life and the Legend*. New York: Alfred A. Knopf, 1976.

Rountree, Helen C. *Pocahontas, Powhatan, Opechancanough: Three Indian Lives Changed by Jamestown*. Charlottesville: University of Virginia Press, 2005.

———. *Pocahontas's People: The Powhatan Indians of Virginia Through Four Centuries*. Norman: University of Oklahoma Press, 1996.

Tilton, Robert S. *Pocahontas: The Evolution of an American Narrative*. New York: Cambridge University Press, 1994.

Townsend, Camilla. *Pocahontas and the Powhatan Dilemma*. New York: Hill and Wang, 2004.

PHOTO CREDITS: Cover—Barbara Marvis; pp. 1, 3—John Langston; pp. 4, 6—Getty Images; p. 8—Library of Congress; p. 12—Hulton Archives; p. 14—Superstock; p. 16—Carly Peterson; p. 17—Jamestown Amusement & Vending Co., Inc.; p. 18—Getty Images; p. 21—Jean Leon Gerome Ferris; p. 22—John Gadsby Chapman; p. 23—Henry Brueckner; p. 24—William L. Sheppard; p. 27—Kings Lynn Museum.

On the Internet

Colonial National Historical Parks; Pocahontas: Her Life and Her Legend
  http://www.nps.gov/archive/colo/Jthanout/Pocahnts.html
Historic Jamestowne
  http://www.historicjamestowne.org/
Jamestown 1607: Windows to the New World
  http://www.jamestown107.org/
Jamestown Rediscovery
  http://www.apva.org/jr.html
Powhatan Renape Nation
  http://www.powhatan.org/
The Real Pocahontas, by David Morenus
  http://pocahontas.morenus.org/
Virtual Jamestown: "Powhatan"
  http://www.virtualjamestown.org/Powhat1.html
Werowocomoco Research Project
  http://powhatan.wm.edu/

GLOSSARY

baptized (BAP-tyzd)—Formally became a Christian and accepted a Christian name.
bushel (BUH-shul)—A unit of measure for dry goods, such as dried corn and beans, that in modern times equals 32 quarts.
cannon (KAN-un)—A mounted gun.
copper (KAH-pur)—A reddish brown metal that's easy to mold but keeps its shape when heated.
elder (EL-der)—A wise and respected, but older, member of a community.
grindstone (GRYND-stohn)—A large stone used to crush dried corn.
hardship (HARD-ship)—Something that makes life unpleasant or difficult.
pneumonia (noo-MOH-nyuh)—A disease of the lungs that causes fever and makes it difficult to breathe.
sacred (SAY-kred)—Used only for religious purposes.
tuberculosis (too-bur-kyoo-LOH-sis)—A disease of the lungs that has some of the same symptoms as pneumonia.
warrior (WAR-ee-er)—A person trained to fight in battle.

INDEX

Amonute (*see* Pocahontas, names of)
Argall, Samuel 20, 21–22
Chesapeake Bay 4, 7, 16
Christianity 21, 22, 23
corn 6, 7, 9, 15, 19
England 4, 5, 16, 20, 24, 25–26
Fort James (Jamestown) 4, 6, 7, 11, 12, 15, 16, 17, 18, 20, 23, 26, 27
galleons 26
guns 5, 15, 20–21
Henrico 21
James River 16
Kocoum 20
London 25
Newport (Captain Christopher) 5
Pacific Ocean 13
Pocahontas
  in artwork 8, 17, 21, 22, 23, 24
  baptism of 22
  child of 23
  childhood of 5–7, 8, 9–11, 13, 16, 17
  death of 26, 27
  in England 24, 25–26
  family of 5–6, 9, 10–11,
  friendships of 11, 13, 15, 17, 18, 19
  kidnapping of 20, 21
  marriages of 20, 22, 23
  names of 10, 17, 22, 25
  saves Smith's life 8, 10–11
Powhatan (chief) 5–6, 9–11, 13, 15, 19, 20, 21, 22, 25–26
Powhatan (people) 4, 5–7, 9–11, 16, 17, 18, 20–21
raccoons 10, 11
Rebecca (*see* Pocahontas, names of)
Richmond 16
Rolfe, John 21–22, 23, 25, 26, 27
Rolfe, Thomas 23, 25, 26, 27
Smith, John (Captain) 7, 8, 9–11, 12, 13, 15, 19, 26, 27
trading 7, 11, 15, 16, 18
village life (Powhatan) 9, 11, 14, 15, 20
Virginia 16, 27
Williamsburg 16
York River 16, 17

JUN 16 2011

25⁷⁰